Old Cumbernauld with Condorrat and

by Guthrie Hutton

These houses off Laird's Hill and Braeface Road were built with a view of open countryside to the north, but the slopes opposite have now been filled with housing. The newly planted trees have also grown to maturity since 1968 when the picture was taken from the walkway under Seafar Road.

© 2007 Guthrie Hutton
First published in the United Kingdom, 2007,
by Stenlake Publishing Ltd.
www.stenlake.co.uk
ISBN 9781840334029

The new town centre was less than ten years old when this picture was taken in 1975 and described as an 'airy circulation space channelling pedestrian movement', but fashions change over time, in buildings as in other things.

ACKNOWLEDGEMENTS

Compiling a small local history like this is like an adventure; you never know what you will encounter along the way and Cumbernauld certainly threw up some challenges. I am grateful to those who helped me to overcome these. Oxfam granted permission to use the picture on the inside back cover. The Robert Gordon University, Aberdeen provided some excellent pictures of the new town on pages 1, 2, 44, 46, 47 and 48. The picture on page 45 was taken by or for Gillespie, Kidd and Coia but, despite a search, we were unable to discover from whom to obtain permission and would thus be pleased to hear from anyone who can help. The back cover picture was provided courtesy of the Royal Commission on the Ancient and Historical Monuments of Scotland (Wheeler & Sproson Collection). I am grateful to Dianne Watters of the RCAHMS and to Miles Glendinning for their assistance. I am indebted to Dr Louise Yeoman for her help in unravelling the church history of the village, and to villager Andrew Burnett, who shared his memories during a chance encounter. The staffs of Kilsyth, Cumbernauld, Falkirk and Kirkintilloch Libraries, and the Mitchell Library, Glasgow, were also helpful in tracking down those elusive details. I must also thank the *Cumbernauld News* for publishing an appeal for help.

FURTHER READING

Glendinning, Miles (ed.), *Rebuilding Scotland: The Postwar Vision 1945–1975*, 1997.
Millar, Hugo B., *Historical Cumbernauld*, 1968.
Robertson, Anne S., *The Antonine Wall*, 1960 + reprints.
Sanderson, Kenneth W., *The Scottish Refractory Industry 1830–1980*, 1990.

INTRODUCTION

Cumbernauld new town attracts so much attention it's easy to forget that a village of the same name pre-dated it, although by how much is not known. Its beginnings may date from when the Antonine Wall, the Roman Empire's most northerly frontier, was built along the ridge to the north, but if history played a part, so too did geography. Nestling in a sheltered spot beside a small burn, the village also sat at the junction of two principal roads as they converged on the gap carved through the high ground by the Red Burn. Commerce flowed along these roads, but so did conflict. There was a Roman fort at Castlecary and in later years landowning families built castles at Castlecary and Cumbernauld. The soldiers of Robert the Bruce, the army of Bonnie Prince Charlie, and nineteenth-century political activists all came this way to do battle.

The Cumbernauld villagers watched them pass, and got on with the everyday struggle of a small rural community. Weaving became the principal occupation of ordinary people and a huge fireclay industry became established in the latter part of the nineteenth century. To the south, Condorrat was also a weaving community until that was supplanted by the extractive industries of quarrying and coal mining.

No doubt the story of these villages would have matched that of neighbouring communities had it not been for the passing of the New Towns Act of 1946. In the same year the Clyde Valley Regeneration Plan recommended that 500,000 people should leave the overcrowded centre of Glasgow, but because only half that number could be accommodated within the city limits, the other 250,000 would have to be moved out. Glasgow did not want to lose its population, but four sites were identified: Bishopton, Cumbernauld, Houston and East Kilbride, which became the first new town when work started there in 1947. Two years later Houston was selected, but objections from Greenock and Port Glasgow, and the potential loss of valuable farm land, stopped that idea.

With Glasgow still overcrowded, a Conservative government was elected in 1951. Tories, generally, had concerns about the cost of new towns and their impact on existing communities, so it was a surprise when the Secretary of State for Scotland, James Stuart, pushed for the creation of another new town in 1953. Cumbernauld was preferred because the ground had less agricultural value and by this time Glasgow had come to recognise the benefits, so progress towards putting the legislation in place was relatively quick. Following a brief public inquiry, the order came into force in December 1955. A Development Corporation, appointed the following February, began planning for a scheme that would absorb the old villages, numerous farms and a scattering of houses. Some of these disappeared; others survived as a bold new concept in urban living developed around them.

The town was well established by 1996 when the Development Corporation was wound up. Some parts have matured well, others less so, and while criticism of the once acclaimed centre has kept Cumbernauld in the news, it has also shown that, like any relatively long-established community, the town is thriving and evolving.

Thought to date from the late seventeenth or early eighteenth centuries, this sundial used to stand in the Cumbernauld House rose garden, but when that was turned into a car park by the new town Development Corporation, the sundial was moved.

It is difficult to be precise about when this view of the village from the south-west was taken, but it pre-dates the school extension of 1904. The original school, seen on the right, was opened by the School Board in May 1875. It was built in response to the Education Act of 1872, which required all children between the ages of five and thirteen to attend school. Prior to that there were some non-parochial schools in the area, and the church provided a parish school, thought to have been located at Roadside, which in the 1830s was catering for 80 to 90 pupils. The new school had some 300 children on the roll by 1900 and they were being taught by nine teachers. Twenty years later secondary education up to third year was being provided, although this was scaled back to junior secondary status in 1940, and just before work started on the new town the school was catering for some 70 junior secondary and 250 primary pupils. It is now closed.

The school is on the left of this view of the village taken from the direction of Wilderness Brae. The picture also shows the backs of houses in Main Street with their gardens running down towards the Old Glasgow Road in the foreground. These long, narrow strips of ground were typical of old Scottish towns, providing householders with land on which they could grow food. They were known as riggs, or in Cumbernauld the Lang Riggs. These walled enclosures survived into the twentieth century as a fine example of medieval Scots town layout, but when the village was modernised as part of the new town, the area was landscaped into a common parkland which has since suffered from vandalism.

A Royal Commission, set up to investigate the state of housing in Scotland, gave an impetus to the provision of public housing when it reported in 1917 on the dreadful condition some people were living in. Thus stirred, councils set about condemning sub-standard, privately owned accommodation and erecting their own housing stock. The first council houses in Cumbernauld village, in Stirling Street, were built in 1927 and are seen here in December of that year, with merrily smoking chimneys indicating occupancy. The scheme was extended in 1930 when the houses in neighbouring Wigtoun Place were erected, and another 21 houses in Longwill Terrace were built in 1939. After the Second World War a further scheme of 54 houses was completed in Auld and Carrick Roads. More council houses were erected near Cumbernauld Station and 190 were built at Condorrat.

Although Cumbernauld's Lodge St Andrew No. 199 dated back to 1797, it did not have dedicated premises until 1906, when the Masonic Temple, on the left of this picture, was built in Glasgow Road, opposite the school. The quantity of materials lying in front of the building suggests that this picture was taken during construction. The foundation stone was laid in early June following a parade through the village which seemed to attract most of the villagers. It was led by the Dennyloanhead Pipe Band and included the Cumbernauld Silver Band and the Cumbernauld Section of the Kirkintilloch Company 1st Dumbartonshire Rifle Volunteers. A jar containing local and national newspapers and other items of interest of the day was placed in a cavity in the stone. The completed Temple was consecrated in late December and from early in 1907 it became a central element of village life, hosting a variety of meetings and functions.

There had been a Catholic church in the village for over 300 years until it was vacated at the time of the Reformation in 1560. For nearly a century after that churchgoers from Cumbernauld had to trek to the parish church at Oxgang near Lenzie, a walk that got longer in 1644 when their place of worship was moved to Kirkintilloch Cross. This was clearly a disincentive and so, in 1649, the church authorities split the parish in two with the names Wester and Easter Lenzie, which were later renamed Kirkintilloch and Cumbernauld Parishes. The good folk of Cumbernauld moved quickly and within a year they had erected a church on the ruins of the former Catholic Church. A new wing was added in 1659 and the whole structure was elevated by another storey at the end of the eighteenth century. Following the Disruption, the schism that split the Established Church of Scotland in 1843, Cumbernauld found itself served by three churches, but the old one survived, becoming known for a time as St Ninian's, before outlasting the breakaway churches and taking the more venerable title of Old Parish Church.

The western end of the main road running through the old village is named Baronhill, a name thought to derive from feudal times when the Baron-Baillie, the representative of baronial power and civic authority, may have lived here. The name is also a good example of how risky it can be to interpret history through place-names, because old maps, newspapers and postcards (including this one) often referred to the area as 'Barnhill', which could lead the unwary to an entirely different conclusion. Whatever the name's origins, the street would simply have been home to the people who lived there, as this picture from 1927 shows. It was used as a postcard by the woman standing in front of the cottage just to the right of centre. She sent it to her niece Cathie, in Glasgow, with the message, 'Do you see me with wee Tommy at the door?' You can imagine the thrill, in the days when cameras were a luxury, of having a picture postcard produced not only showing your street, but you and your house as well – good business for the publisher, Miss Livingstone, who ran the post office along with her grocery shop.

Almost certainly taken at the same time as the photograph on page 9, this picture shows Main Street looking towards Baronhill. The solitary car could even have been the photographer's own vehicle strategically parked to give a little foreground interest. On the right are the premises of the Cumbernauld Co-operative Society, which was set up around 1860. Being a small local society, it struggled in the shadow of the much larger Kilsyth Co-op, which was famous for its generous dividends. Frequent proposals for amalgamation failed to get the necessary majority until 1933, when a large vote in favour set the wheels in motion, but the members rejected the proposed terms and conditions a few months later and Cumbernauld Co-op carried on. This shop, on the corner of Main Street and Smithyends, appears to have dealt in drapery, clothing and footwear, though latterly it sold hardware. The Co-op had other premises on the corner of The Wynd and Main Street where groceries were sold.

The most remarkable thing about the village is how little it has actually changed, although the absence of motor cars in this picture of Main Street, from December 1927, makes it look like another place. Of course there are differences, but many of these are cosmetic and, compared to other Scottish towns and villages, the townscape is still substantially as it was. The principal reason for this is that when Cumbernauld was chosen as the site for a new town the village was left alone while the Development Corporation concentrated on their main task. Then in 1965 they appointed the architect Philip S. Cocker to draw up plans which allowed the village to develop but preserved its essential character. Some buildings were restored, while others were virtually rebuilt behind their existing frontages in a scheme commended by the Royal Fine Arts Commission. There is a delicious irony in this, because much of Scotland's urban landscape was trashed in the 1960s by over-zealous councillors and planners, and there will be many places in the country envious of the way new Cumbernauld treated the old.

Smithyends is seen here looking north from Main Street around 1905 in a picture which shows the uneven road width and irregular building line that existed before the new town redevelopment. Smithyends, and The Wynd further east, follow the line of riggs which existed on the north side of Main Street as well as to the south (see page 5). It is possible that these streets may originally have been little more than lanes, with access to them being through a close or pend, and that over time, as the main road to the north of the village was improved and the village expanded, they would have been widened and opened up to Main Street. Smithyends, or as it was formerly known, Smithyinns, is presumed to have been named after a blacksmith's forge, while the 'inns' part of the earlier name could refer to a common close rather than a public house.

Smithyends is seen here around 1910 looking back towards Main Street, with a little row of cottages on the left made up of what looks like single ends or room and kitchen dwellings. There are only women and children standing outside – which suggests that the men are at work – and the cottages are typical of industrial housing at the time, although it is not known what if any connection they had to a local works. The little row jutted out beyond the line of other houses in the street, as can be seen more clearly in the picture on the opposite page. These houses have since been removed, while other cottages closer to Roadside remain in existence, surrounded by housing erected on former rigg lands as part of the new town development. This particular scheme won a Saltire Society Award in 1969.

It is possible that this picture of Main Street was taken in June 1906 at the same time as the foundation stone of the Masonic Temple in Glasgow Road was laid, because on that occasion flags were strung across the road from the Masonic Arms (now The Villager pub) to the bank. The street seems quiet, as if the villagers are waiting for something to happen or drawing breath after festivities. Two delivery vans are parked in the street. The one in the distance belonged to Robert Brown, family baker, while that on the extreme left is outside William Watson's bakery. Watson's were still using a horse-drawn van in 1921 when Andrew M. Watson was thrown off and injured. He had been driving along Back o' Bog Road at South Cumbernauld when a passing motor lorry frightened the animal, which bolted, causing the vehicles to crash.

This picture, taken at much the same time as the one on the opposite page, shows almost the same section of Main Street, but looking the other way. The Masonic Arms, with its distinctive street-facing gable, is in the background, as is Robert Brown's bakery van. Another delivery van is seen on the left-hand side of the street outside the Cross Keys pub, which has now been renamed after another old village hostelry, the Black Bull. The original Black Bull had been a town house of the Wigton family before Cumbernauld House was built in 1731. It had become a public house by 1746 when the Jacobite general, Lord George Murray, lodged there when the section of Bonnie Prince Charlie's army he commanded billeted itself at Cumbernauld before the Battle of Falkirk. The actual building appears to have been replaced in the nineteenth century and its location forgotten until redevelopment in 1966 uncovered cellars at 61 Main Street thought to be those of the famous old pub.

The Wynd probably began as little more than a narrow lane linking the main east–west thoroughfares through the village. Some evidence for the way in which it developed was discovered in 1965 during a survey done as part of the redevelopment of the village. Houses at numbers 33 and 35 were found to have back walls dating from the seventeenth century and fronts from around 1800, showing that there may have been some regularising of the street line at that time. There is also evidence of different periods of building in the view of this street which is shown on the front cover, with the crow-stepped gables of some buildings suggesting an earlier construction than the arched pend in the right foreground, which is dated 1836. The Wynd has also been known in the past as Bridge Street or Church Street, the former because it crossed the, now culverted, Back Burn at its junction with the main road, and the latter because of the church, with its distinctive tower, on the left. Both bridge and church are seen on the opposite page in a picture from around 1905.

The church at the north end of The Wynd came about because some churchmen were so concerned about state patronage and the diminished role of presbytery in the Established Church of Scotland that they left in 1733 to form the first Secession Church. The Cumbernauld congregation was formed in 1737 and appears to have worshipped with one from Falkirk until 1743, when a church was established in the village. This was almost certainly in The Wynd, where the front wall of the existing structure has a stone plaque declaring it to have been built in 1743 and rebuilt in 1825. Church history, however, is rarely cast in stone and in 1839 the minister and congregation rejoined the Established Church, only to leave it again four years later during the Disruption, a dispute which saw large numbers of ministers, with some or all of their congregations, leave the Establishment to form the Free Church. In 1900 the Free Church amalgamated with other dissenting churches to form the United Free Church. The church in The Wynd became the Bridgend United Free Church, and when its congregation amalgamated with that of the Baird Church at the foot of Main Street in 1920, it was renamed St Andrews.

Distant views of a town can look unexciting and so, in the pictures on these two pages, the photographer has artfully added interest by filling the foregrounds with the same three children. He (it probably was a he) has not moved much between shots, which has had the effect of creating a panoramic picture of what the village looked like from the west and north (the circled building shows where the views overlap). The pictures were taken around 1906 from a spot between Mainhead and Carrickstone Farms, an area which has now largely been consumed by modern housing, although the spot where the children have been put would have been either on or close to the present-day main A80 road.

The stone which Carrickstone Farm was named after sits behind a battered old fence, beside a footpath which itself traces the line of an old road that used to run across the ridge. Although now surrounded by housing, it is clear that the site of the stone once commanded the countryside, because a former Ordnance Survey triangulation pillar and a water tower sit alongside it. The Carrick Stone has been likened to a Roman altar and its name linked to King Robert the Bruce, who was also Earl of Carrick. This is based on the supposed military advantage that Bruce would have gained from occupying the high ground, possibly to besiege Cumbernauld Castle, to conduct manoeuvres before the Battle of Bannockburn, or to raise his standard before the battle. These are, however, somewhat speculative theories and the real origins of the stone and its name remain unknown.

This fine run of buildings known as Parkview, which is also shown on the right of the previous page, was at the southern end of Roadside. Although occupied by sitting tenants, it was put up for sale in March 1928, when it was described as a substantial tenement of two storeys and attics. The ground attached to each title was expressed in old units of measure as one rood, six falls and twelve ells. The terrace presumably got its Parkview name because it had an uninterrupted view of the park, or field, directly in front – in Scotland an enclosed field was commonly referred to as a park. After the Second World War a group of sixteen 'prefabs' – prefabricated houses – were built on the other side of the road, at which point a more accurate name would have been 'Prefab View'. Terrace and prefabs have both since been demolished.

Roadside, seen here at its northern end, is an interesting name implying a thoroughfare of some importance, and so it was. In the mid-eighteenth century Scotland's roads were dreadful and the government sought to improve them by authorising the construction of turnpike roads. These were not built by the state, but by private investors who obtained an Act of Parliament, which also permitted them to charge tolls to recoup their outlay: the 'turnpike' was the toll gate. One such road was the main north–south highway to and from Glasgow which was taken round the north of the village, bypassing the original high street. When the main road was subsequently rerouted to the south of the village, Roadside became a back street. Modern road developments have since turned its northern end into a cul-de-sac, where the former manse of the United Presbyterian Church has become the local branch of the Royal Bank of Scotland, known as Baird House.

Situated at a major road junction, the Spur Hotel, formerly the Cumbernauld Inn, was well placed as a coaching inn and posting house. The village name was inscribed on the corner of the building facing the road junction and, as this picture from around 1910 shows, this was augmented by other signage. The large building behind the inn was the 'Baird' Church, which was used by a congregation formed around 1758 after a division in the Secession Church. Such splits had largely healed by 1849 when the United Presbyterian Church was formed, although only this of the two secession congregations in Cumbernauld joined the new church. The building seen here was erected in 1860 to seat 350 people and was named after Hugh Baird, the minister at that time. In 1900 the United Presbyterian and Free Churches came together as the United Free Church and in 1920 the congregations of the Baird and Bridgend Churches amalgamated. The Baird Church was vacated and a drapery and fish restaurant were opened in it; the restaurant outlasted the clothes shop, but only until 1926 when the building became the Bradford Cinema. It has now been demolished.

When it became clear that the bodies of men killed in the First World War would not be brought home for burial, the people of Cumbernauld Parish, in common with the rest of the country, were moved to remember them in a communal way. A public meeting was held in July 1919, presided over by Captain Alan Burns, at which ideas for a memorial were put forward and a committee set up to make final recommendations. They proposed a simple cross, which was erected beside the bowling green, opposite the Spur Hotel. It was unveiled on 22 May 1921 by Lieutenant Colonel Sir Iain Colquhoun of Luss, Lord Lieutenant of Dunbartonshire. The Cumbernauld Silver Band played a lament and wreaths were laid, including a beautiful one of forget-me-nots from Cumbernauld estate and Captain and Mrs Burns. Captain Burns, who presided over the ceremony, handed the memorial over to the Parish Council for upkeep. It has since been moved to Baronhill.

Of all the transport routes that throughout history have converged on Castlecary, the one that made the greatest visual impact was the Edinburgh & Glasgow Railway, opened in 1842. It took a less than direct route across the country so that the track could be laid as level as possible and thus allow the early locomotives to travel as fast as they could. To achieve this, the engineers had to build up huge embankments, excavate cuttings and tunnels, and construct some magnificent viaducts, including one of eight arches across the valley of the Red Burn. It is seen here from the original A80 Stirling Road as it passes through Castlecary village. The viaduct was undoubtedly an imposing structure, but it came at a cost; the tracks were driven straight across the site of the Roman fort, to take advantage of the optimum line for the railway to bridge the valley.

Castlecary Station was situated just west of the viaduct and was one of the original stations on the line, with connecting coach services to Stirling. Its importance diminished as other lines opened up and it latterly just served the village, closing in 1967. It was the scene of a number of accidents, the worst of which occurred in a snowstorm in December 1937, when an express ran into a stationary train, killing 35 people. Behind the station, on the right, is the Castlecary Fireclay and Lime Works, which was started around 1883 by an Alexander Weir. Its lime-making activities, which exploited local limestone, ceased after the First World War and thereafter the works concentrated on making firebricks. It struggled through the 1920s and became part of the Glenboig Union Fireclay Company in 1936. When the plant closed in 1968 some of the workforce moved to another brickworks located to the east of the railway viaduct. Initially operated by one of the giants of the fireclay industry, John G. Stein, that works also closed around 1980.

The so-called 'Roman Bridge', seen in the foreground of this picture, spanned the Red Burn, just to the east of Castlecary Station. It acquired its popular name for obvious reasons – it was old, ruinous and close to the Roman fort at Castlecary – but it was not Roman and was most likely built for the eighteenth-century turnpike road. At that time the art of building skew arches had not been learned, so the road builders would have taken advantage of the burn's change of direction just upstream to make their crossing at this point. Others followed: through the arch can be seen the piers of the railway viaduct and the bridge carrying the old A80 main road, which has since been superseded by the culvert carrying the realigned road and A80 dual carriageway. In Roman times there was a road running behind the Antonine Wall which would have had to cross the burn, but it is not known if this was by a bridge or a ford.

The original part of Castle Cary was built around 1478 by a junior branch of the Livingstone family of Callender, Falkirk, to protect them from the predations of their neighbours, the Flemings of Cumbernauld. The castle stood on a bank above the Red Burn close to the Castlecary Roman fort, which seems to have been used as a ready source of cut stone by the castle's builders. The castle appears to have been extended before 1640, when it became the property of the Baillie family. They must have rued being related to General Baillie, whose Covenanting army was beaten by Montrose at the Battle of Kilsyth in 1645. The victorious soldiery pursued the general to the castle, but he got away, so they torched the castle instead. The damage was made good and the castle remained occupied, becoming part of the Dundas family estates in the mid-nineteenth century. A century later, local antiquary Hugo Millar was living in it and trying to restore its former glory.

A Cumbernauld Castle had existed for some time before the Fleming family took over the property in the fourteenth century. As staunch supporters of the Stuart cause, they prospered, building up the castle and also attaining the Earldom of Wigton, but such connections could have their downside. Oliver Cromwell's army moved into Scotland in 1650, defeating the Royalists at Dunbar and consolidating their hold on the country by reducing to ruin their supporters' castles. Cumbernauld Castle was one of these and the site remained derelict until 1731, when the 6th Earl of Wigton built a magnificent house where the old castle had stood. It was designed by the great Scottish architect William Adam, father of the perhaps more famous Robert Adam. The house may not have been completed as intended, because it has two pavilions to the left of the main house and none on the right, which is odd given the taste for symmetry at the time.

This curious building, known as the 'gamekeeper's house', stood near the east gate of Cumbernauld House until around 1960 when it was demolished. Tucked in behind it on the left of the picture is a circular dovecote (or doocot), which was incorporated into the estate's walled garden. Landowners were allowed under feudal law to keep pigeons as a source of food, and doocots of various shapes and sizes can be seen throughout the country. This one is thought to be contemporary with the big house. Cumbernauld House itself was destroyed internally by a fire in 1877 and the Adam interiors were not remade when the house was reinstated. It was sold in 1955 by its then owner, Colonel John Burns, and became the headquarters of Cumbernauld Development Corporation, an oddly classical setting for a body dedicated to modernity. It was also ironic that those charged with delivering the egalitarian concept of a new town should be referred to by scornful tenants as 'them up at the big hoose', just as earlier occupants had been.

Although now used for prosaic functions like water filtration, the lovely, steep-sided, wooded glens formed by the Red Burn and its tributaries have long been popular scenic attractions. This bridge appears to have been on a well-used path between the grounds of Cumbernauld House and Abronhill, and has since been replaced by a more modern structure. Woodlands once made Cumbernauld famous as one of last places where the ancient Caledonian forest survived. The forest was also regarded as the last habitat of the native white cattle which, according to a sixteenth-century chronicler, had long manes like 'fierce lions', 'were more wild than any other beasts', and when hunted had 'no fear of hounds, sharp lances or other penetrative weapons'. Alas, this reputation did not deter those who pursued them for game and even in the 1570s the king was being criticised for actions which endangered the survival of the species. With such an early example of concern for wildlife, Cumbernauld must have a claim to be the cradle of conservationism.

This little row of cottages, lying to the south-west of Cumbernauld House at the top of Wilderness Brae, was known, appropriately, as Braehead. As the new town developed in the early 1960s the row was turned into a little local theatre named the Cottage Theatre, run by members of the Cumbernauld Theatre Group. It put on some ambitious productions, but inevitably the size of the venue limited its scope. In the 1970s Cumbernauld Theatre Trust took over from the early Cottage Theatre group and, with funding from Cumbernauld Development Corporation, Cumbernauld and Kilsyth District Council and the Scottish Arts Council, the building was expanded. The new theatre included two auditoria of 300 and 80 seats, rehearsal rooms, bar, restaurant and front-of-house facilities, while retaining the Braehead cottage frontage.

The houses on the right of this picture, looking south around 1910, were part of a hamlet known as South Muirhead, which joined the list of Scotland's lost villages when the new town was built. The little road it was on effectively formed the spine of the new town. It left a junction with the old A73 near Kildrum Farm, ran across the ridge where Cumbernauld new town centre was built and went past Seafar Farm, before joining up with other minor roads to the south-west of Greenfaulds. The section of road seen here is now approximately where South Muirhead Road runs from the Royal Mail depot to the police station, with Pizza Hut in between.

It was not unusual for early stations to be some distance from the place they purported to serve, and as often as not a new community developed around the railway. At Cumbernauld this had grown to sufficient size by the late nineteenth century for a school to be built which could accommodate 50 pupils up to the age of eight, taught by two teachers. Known variously as the Southern District or Cumbernauld Station School, it still had its full complement of children in the 1950s when the occupants of a scheme of 54 council houses had added to the local population. The picture shows the school around 1910, with Station Road heading off in the direction of Cumbernauld village. In the centre of the background is Carbrain Farm, which was demolished to make way for the new town.

The Scottish Central Railway was opened in 1848. It was a remarkably visionary line, running up the spine of the country from a southern terminal in what was then a field in the middle of nowhere, but is now Greenhill, near Bonnybridge. Sceptics scoffed, but the ambitious Caledonian Railway Company saw its potential. Seeking to extend their Carlisle to Glasgow main line, they acquired two early Lanarkshire concerns, the Wishaw & Coltness and Garnkirk & Glasgow Railways. These lines gave the Caledonian access to the north side of Glasgow, but by also laying a ten-mile-long connection from the Coatbridge area to butt on to the end of the Scottish Central, they were able to run through trains to the north of Scotland. The Castlecary Branch, as it was known, opened in August 1848. A station, about a mile and half from Cumbernauld village, was initially established along with the line, although it did not fully open for passenger traffic until around 1870.

With the new town being sited on a hill top and designed around the motor car, the railway was left on the edge of the town. This failure to incorporate the station as a central element of the plan looks in hindsight to have been (at best) a missed opportunity, particularly as the suburban rail network around Glasgow was electrified in the early 1960s and the Cumbernauld line was left out of the scheme. That people are keen to use train services is borne out by the opening of a new station at Greenfaulds in the 1980s, and more recently in the steady expansion of the town in the direction of Croy Station and its enlarged car park. Now also modernised, Cumbernauld Station is seen here from a passing train in 1962, before Cumbernauld High School was built on the rising ground which can be seen in the distance between the tree and the little shed.

The station village is seen here from the approximate location of the present-day Lenziemill Industrial Estate. The Southern District hall and post office are on the right with, between them, a minor road – on the line of the present B8054, Lenziemill Road – which crossed the main road, although the picture does not show this clearly. Perhaps drivers in the early days of motoring also found the junction hard to see, because accidents occurred here regularly. Around the turn of the nineteenth and twentieth centuries a homeless man settled in this vicinity. Known as Long Haired Sam, his doleful countenance was framed by long, matted black hair which he never brushed, combed or cut. Apparently, as a university student in the 1880s, he was engaged to a young woman, but she jilted him, causing him to give up his studies and take to the road. He stopped wandering when he reached Cumbernauld, but although he did odd jobs and errands for people – who rewarded him with food and somewhere to sleep – he remained reclusive and very sad. The hall was run by a local committee and used for a variety of functions, including church services. The post office-cum-shop was a regular target of petty thieves, but between them the two buildings provided a focus for local people, many of whom would have been employed in the Cumbernauld Brick and Pipe Works, the chimneys of which can be seen between the two buildings.

Heading north in 1945, this train has just left the station and is passing the Cumbernauld Brick and Pipe works on the left. The works was started in 1874 by the Cumbernauld Fire-Clay Company, who used clay mined at Abronhill. They sold the works in 1882 to the Glenboig Union Fireclay Company, who started to exploit seams of fireclay in Glencryan. Tubs of clay were hauled from the Palacerigg Mine, as it was known, by a continuous cable worked from an engine at the works. The clay was particularly suited for making items like salt-glazed water pipes, chimney cans, ridge tiles, wall copings, troughs and ornamental garden ware. At its peak the enterprise employed 80 men and women with another 20 at the mine. The clay mine was worked out by 1958, but the works kept going, using imported clay, until 1969.

Glencryan Burn flows down to the Red Burn from Fannyside Loch, a shallow moorland lochan, where these evidently well-to-do people are enjoying some winter sport – even the family chauffeur has entered into the fun. Fannyside Moor was always important to local people as a source of cut peat for winter fuel. Much of this was done to the west of the loch at Palacerigg, where a farm colony was set up in 1907 to provide work for unemployed men from Glasgow.

About 90 men stayed on site in hutted accommodation while hundreds more arrived daily by train from the city. The residential element ceased in the 1930s, but buses continued to bring the men to the site up to the Second World War, when the scheme ceased. The area, taking in Glencryan, Palacerigg and up to Fannyside, has now been incorporated into the Palacerigg Country Park.

Although almost a mile due south of Cumbernauld Station, Luggiebank, seen here in pictures from the early and mid-twentieth century, has the appearance of a railway commuter village from the Victorian era. It was just across the old Dunbartonshire and Lanarkshire county boundary, which ran along the Luggie Water, and this could have had an influence on the siting of the village where it is, and not closer to the station. The road through the village was formerly the A73, which ran between Airdrie and a junction with the A80 at Cumbernauld Village, but with the building of the new town the roads have been routed round Luggiebank and the old main road is now a cul-de-sac. With no traffic crossing the old bridge over the Luggie Water, the riverside has become more secluded and perhaps more attractive to wildlife, which once included kingfishers and otters. Blaes, a shaly mineral used in brick making, was also once worked in the area.

Having been subsumed into Cumbernauld new town, Condorrat has seen big changes, although some elements of this village Main Road, photographed in 1927, are still recognisable, especially the former Co-op store on the right, which is still a small grocery. Originally Condorrat had its own Co-operative Society, but this amalgamated with the Kilsyth Co-operative Society in 1922. A hundred years before that, Cumbernauld Parish had a population of just over 3,000 people whose cottages collectively contained some 500 handlooms. Condorrat, its second largest community, was therefore, unsurprisingly, a weaving village. Working at home, people wove linen cloth which wholesalers from the towns and cities bought and then sold on to retailers. With profits being made at every stage, weavers were not well paid and often lived close to subsistence level. Eventually handlooms were superseded by large steam-powered mills and people had to find other employment, which, for the villagers of Condorrat, was in the coal industry, ironically, perhaps, supplying fuel to drive the mills.

The handloom weavers of Condorrat and elsewhere faced hardship when demand slumped after the Napoleonic wars, a time which also coincided with a rise in political awareness amongst ordinary people. This posed a serious challenge to the authorities in 1820 when the Radicals, as they were known, met in Glasgow to set up a Provisional Government for Scotland. Anxious to protect their movement, an Andrew Hardie and some lightly armed men set out to capture weapons from the Carron Ironworks and recruit workers to the cause. At Condorrat they met up with other Radicals, including John Baird, a weaver who assumed command of the 35-man 'army'. Duped by a government spy, they waited for reinforcements on Bonnymuir, near Bonnybridge, but instead battle-hardened hussars and troopers of the Stirlingshire Militia caught up with them. After a short skirmish, the Radicals surrendered: Baird and Hardie were subsequently hanged. Although ultimately futile, this incident speaks volumes for the weavers of Condorrat that so many were prepared to risk all in an attempt to achieve something we take for granted today – a say in the political process. The building with the dormer windows facing camera in this 1920s picture is believed to be on the site of Baird's cottage. A plaque on the wall commemorates what he did.

This 1920s view of the Main Road to the south of the main village centre is still substantially the same today. The prominent telegraph poles have been replaced by modern street furniture, some houses have been rebuilt, and the new houses of Rosehill Place occupy the ground on the left beside the church. The church itself would have been a major change when it was built in 1875 as a *quoad sacra* parish church of the Church of Scotland. This term meant that the church did not have the full range of parochial responsibilities, but was able to meet the spiritual needs of a sizeable number of people who were not easily served by the existing parish church in Cumbernauld. Such a development reflects a wider change in Condorrat, which was beginning to grow along with the large-scale extractive industries.

A public subscription taken up in the 1830s raised sufficient funds to build a two-roomed dwelling house for the Condorrat schoolmaster, indicating that there was some educational provision in the village before the Education Act of 1872. A couple of years after the Act the newly appointed School Board was presiding over a village school and employing William Kerr as its teacher. Clearly that early school was inadequate to cope with the numbers, because the Condorrat School building in this picture was erected in 1898. It was beside the Main Road at Dalshannon, some distance from the centre of the village, but there was accommodation for 200 pupils and five teachers, one of whom was William Kerr, who remained in post until 1913. This old school has now been superseded and houses have been built on the site.

The architects and planners of Cumbernauld new town, influenced by the ideas of the French architect Le Corbusier, believed that with good design they could create a better living environment than the one the prospective inhabitants would be coming from. They chose to create a compact hilltop town with a strong centre surrounded by separate districts, rather than the self-contained neighbourhoods of earlier new towns. They also decided to segregate traffic by creating fast roads shorn of conventional junctions, and with separate walkways for pedestrians, who would cross roads only by way of an overbridge or underpass – as here at North Carbrain Road. The designated area of 4,150 acres stretched between the villages of Cumbernauld and Condorrat and the initial target population was 50,000 people. This was increased to 70,000 in 1961 and upped again in 1974, when the decision was taken to build to the west of the A80, effectively nullifying the original concept for the town.

Construction of the new town was ceremonially begun at Kildrum Farm in June 1957 when the Secretary of State for Scotland, John Maclay, cut the first sod. The Development Corporation was not fully set up, so Glasgow architects Gillespie, Kidd and Coia were appointed to design Kildrum's first houses, some of which are seen behind these new residents. Kildrum Farm was also where Cumbernauld's first shop was opened, in 1959, along with a branch of the Clydesdale and North of Scotland Bank; a history that helps to explain the survival of the farm buildings amidst all the new housing. Confidence was high at the sod-cutting ceremony: the Burroughs Adding Machine Company had just committed itself to becoming the new town's first major industry, with a predicted workforce of 4,000. By the end of the 1950s the factory at Wardpark was employing over 1,000 people, and in 1967, ten years after the decision to locate in Cumbernauld, the number exceeded 2,700, but it never reached 4,000. Production ceased in the late 1980s and, after a period of use by OKI, the factory was demolished.

The town centre was a huge departure from anything that had gone before, with shops, services and housing all contained within a megastructure built above and around a fast dual carriageway road. It was probably the first covered shopping mall in the country, establishing the concept, but not the bland uniformity of later developments. The first phase was opened in May 1967 by Princess Margaret, who disregarded the carefully planned timetable to chat to local people, look at some shops and inspect St Mungo's Church. She apparently described the centre as 'fabulous', and in those days the structure, designed by Geoffrey Copcutt, was generally regarded as a unique concept in urban living. The American Institute of Architects described it as 'the town centre of the millennium' and in 1967 awarded it the prestigious R. S. Reynolds Memorial Award for Community Architecture. It is seen here in 1968 from the south-eastern pedestrian approach, with the partly hidden sign for Galloway's Supermarket on the right.

This view, also from 1968, shows the centre surmounted by the bowling alley and penthouses. The many-layered and faceted megastructure was originally intended to be half a mile in length, but its construction was stopped after completion of Phase 2 in 1972. Perhaps it was the use of bare concrete – fine in Le Corbusier's France, but grim on a wet and windy Scottish hill top – but when disenchantment with the centre set in, it did so with a vengeance. Confidence seemed to evaporate as scorn and condemnation grew. Buildings erected in the 1970s for the local authority and Inland Revenue made no attempt to relate to it and later town centre phases were just tacked on without reference to the earlier style. It became a visual mess, compounded by the more recent growth of retail sheds. The centre was a brave concept; it may not have worked well, but there is something sad about the way it has become so devalued. Although now partly demolished, it belongs to the country's architectural heritage and deserves some valued recognition.

If the town centre has fared badly in the court of public opinion, some of Cumbernauld's housing has been praised and stands favourable comparison with other new towns or contemporary housing estates, or with what has become fashionable since. The steeply sloping ground at Seafar and Ravenswood, to the north and west of the central ridge, presented difficult terrain for building, but the skilful use of the slope helped to create an attractive urban setting for some very successful house types. It was all enhanced by an excellent planting scheme of mainly native birch and heather, and hard landscaping made up of concrete slabs, naturally occurring rocks and granite setts that formerly paved Glasgow's streets. The area's predominantly two-storeyed dwellings, such as these in Balloch View, sit in stark contrast to Buchan House in the background. It was one of eleven tower blocks built by the Development Corporation as part of a government drive to establish a Scottish prefabricated construction industry.